Kindergarten Success
Number Puzzles

For information about permission to reproduce selections from this book for
an entire school or school district, please contact permissions@highlights.com.

Published by Highlights Learning • 815 Church Street • Honesdale, Pennsylvania 18431
ISBN: 978-1-64472-317-3
Mfg. 02/2021

Printed in Shenzhen, Guangdong, China
First edition
10 9 8 7 6 5 4 3 2

For assistance in the preparation of this book, the editors would like to thank:
Kristin Ward, MS Curriculum, Instruction, and Assessment; K–5 Mathematics Instructional Coach
Jump Start Press, Inc.

Hello!

Draw candles on the cake to show how old you are.

Zero Groceries

Find and circle the shelf that has **0** groceries in it. Find and circle the shopping cart that has **0** groceries in it.

One Bug

Draw a circle around each group that shows 1 bug.
Then draw 1 bug on this flower.

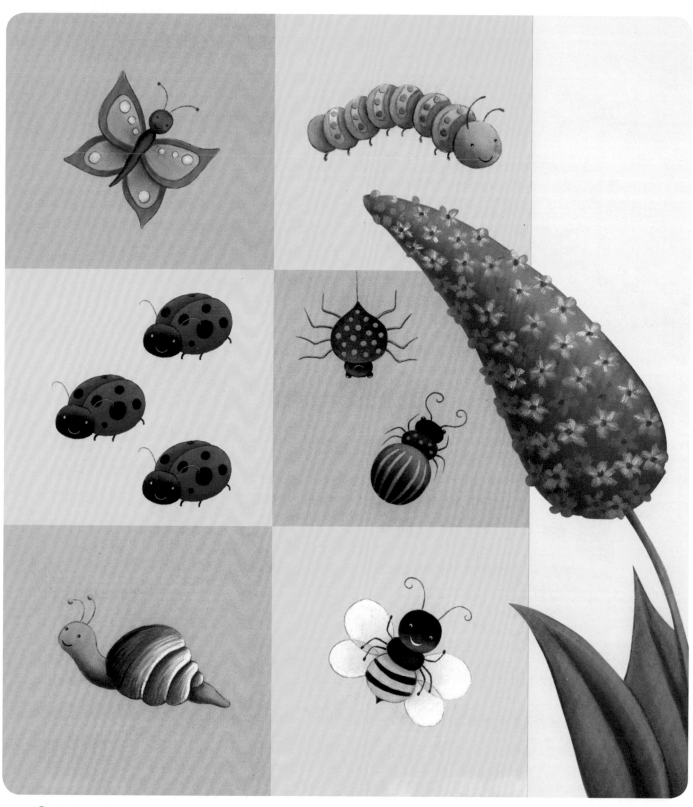

Giddy-Up!

Follow the 1's to help Max and Charlie get back to the barn.

Two Socks

Can you help Sam find his missing sock? Circle it.
Then draw lines to match the other socks in each pair.

A pair equals 2.

Double Diner

Find and circle the **8** objects in this Hidden Pictures puzzle.

How many twins do you see? What other sets of **2** can you find?

BREAKFAST
BACON & EGGS
TOAST & BUTTER
PANCAKES & SYRUP

LUNCH
SOUP & SALAD
MACARONI & CHEESE
PEANUT BUTTER & JELLY

DESSERT
MILK & COOKIES
CAKE & ICE CREAM

kite

boomerang

piece of popcorn

telescope

noodle

butterfly

domino

ice-cream sandwich

Three Paths

Help Opal Owl find her way home to the barn. Then find and circle: 3 🐑 , 3 🐱 , 3 🍎 , and 3 🌾 .

Four Sides

Squares and rectangles have 4 sides. Can you find each of the 4-sided objects in this Hidden Pictures puzzle?

gift

waffle

die

cracker

toast

belt buckle

stamp

window

Five Snacks

Ricky Raccoon is hungry. Follow the directions to help him find **5** kinds of snacks.

Draw O's around 5 .   Draw ☐'s around 5 .

Draw ___'s under 5 ◯.   Draw △'s around 5 ◯.

Draw X's on 5 .

What else can you count 5 of?

Six Hats

Count **6** baseball caps. Then find and circle the **6** objects in this Hidden Pictures puzzle.

boot

hammer

horseshoe

golf club

umbrella

glove

Seven Airplanes

Count the **7** airplanes. Then find the **7** objects in this Hidden Pictures puzzle.

eyeglasse

sailboat

cherry

bow

ruler

horseshoe

lemon

Eight Cats

Count the **8** cats. Then follow the **8**'s to help the mouse reach the cheese.

How many cats do you see?

Nine Ants

Count the **9** ants. Then find and circle the **9** objects in this Hidden Pictures puzzle.

bean

snake

spoon

crown

waffle

olive

comb

baseball bat

mitten

Ten Bikes

Can you find **10** bikes in this picture? Circle each one you find.

Fruitful Fives

Count the pieces of fruit in each rectangle. Draw a line between the pairs of rectangles that together contain **5** pieces of fruit.

Counting: 1, 2, 3, 4, 5

Count Your Chickens

Help Farmer Fran count her chickens. Fill in the number of chickens on each hay bale. Then find and circle the I chicken with a **red** face and the I chicken with an **orange** face.

Eleven Boats

Count the 11 boats. Then find the 11 objects in this Hidden Pictures puzzle.

pencil · dog bone · cane · stamp · slice of pizza · bowling ball · mug · slice of pie · ruler · acorn · doughnut

Flying High

Count the 11 balloons. Then draw a design on the biggest balloon.

Twelve Doughnuts

Count the 12 doughnuts. Then draw lines to connect the matching doughnuts.

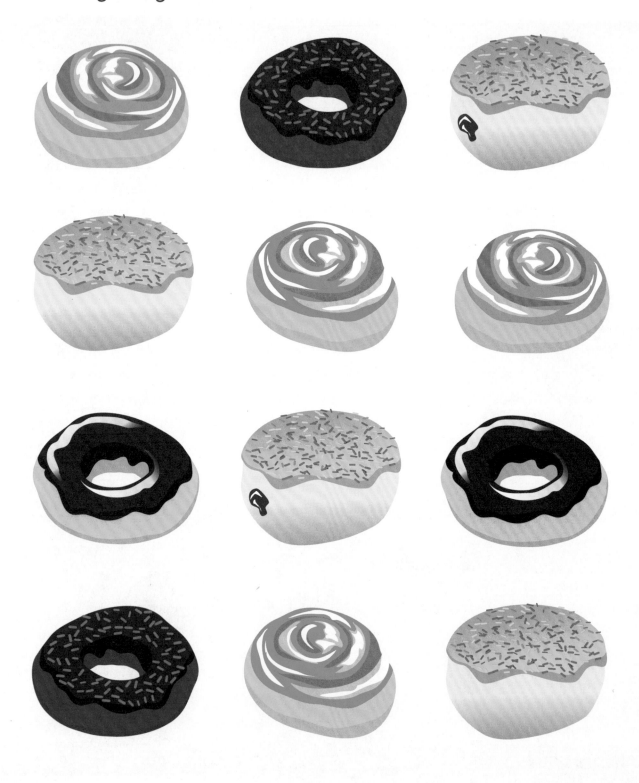

At the Market

Find and circle **12** animals in the top picture.
Then find **12** differences between these pictures.

Thirteen Kids

Count the 13 kids in the top picture. Then find and circle 13 differences between these pictures.

Fourteen Monkeys

Count the 14 monkeys. Then see how many silly things you can find.

PIN the BANANA

Fifteen Butterflies

Count and circle **15** butterflies. Then find the **2** that match.

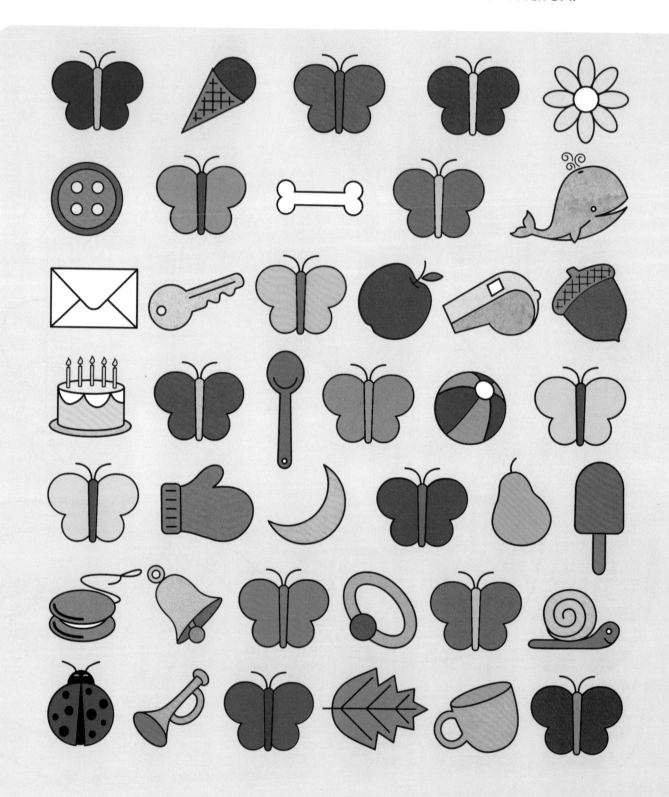

Super Seal

Find and circle **15** differences between these pictures.

Sixteen Leaves

Count the 16 leaves. Then draw a line
from each leaf to its exact match.

Seventeen Bees

Count the bees. Circle the picture that has exactly **17** bees.
Then draw a line between the **2** framed pictures that match.

Remember to cross off as you count.

Eighteen Hedgehogs

Find and circle **18** items that appear in the top picture but are missing from the bottom picture.

Nineteen Balloons

Count and color 19 balloons.

Circle 3 other items that begin with the letter B.

Good Morning!

Connect the dots from 1 to 19 to see someone who lives on a farm.

Twenty Owls

Count the **20** owls. Then find and circle the **10** objects in this Hidden Pictures puzzle.

sailboat   hammer   glove   pineapple   yo-yo   harmonica   straw   bowling ball   crescent moon   wedge of orange

Caterpillar Count

Number Order: 1–20

Fill in the missing numbers from 1 to 20. Then look at the pictures. Can you find at least 12 differences between the 2 pictures?

Toy Match

three

four

two

one

five

Counting: 1–10; Number Words

Count the toys in each group. Then match them with the number word. We did the first one to get you started.

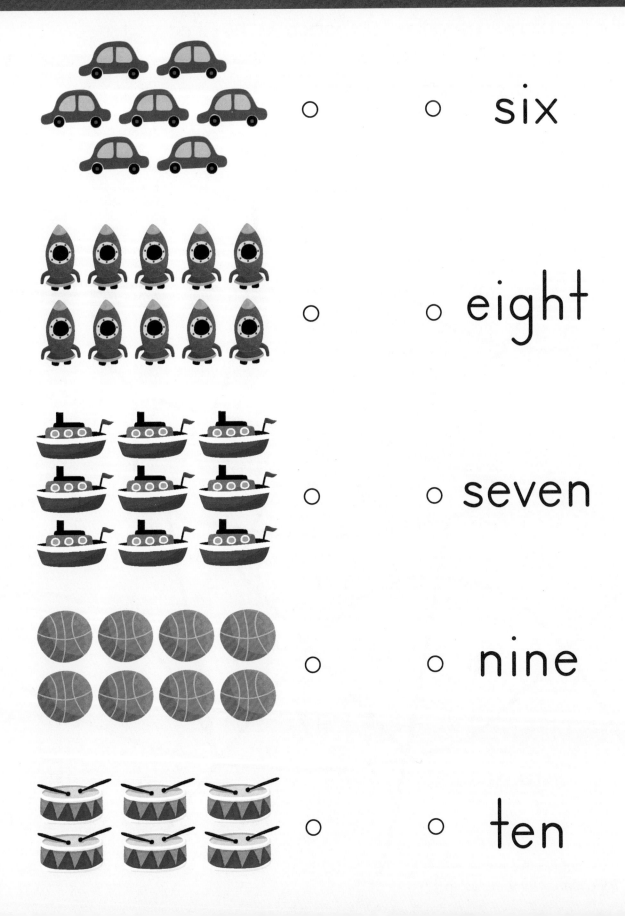

six

eight

seven

nine

ten

What Is It?

Color the picture using the number code. What do you see?
Number Code: 15 = 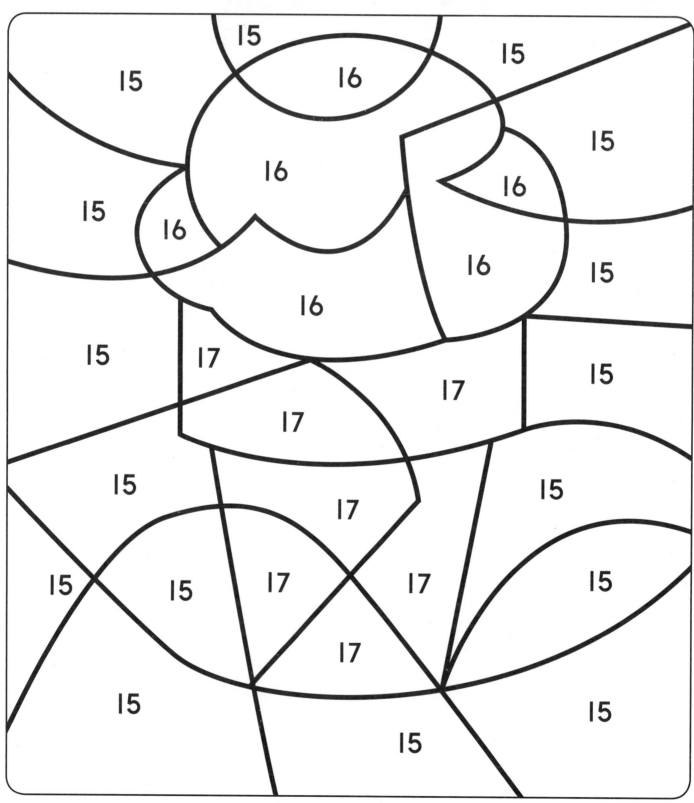 16 = 17 =

Here I Come!

Connect the dots from I to 20 to give this girl a perfect ride.

What is your favorite thing to do at the playground?

A Bunch of Color

Count the dots on each balloon. Color the balloon with **10** dots **red**.
Color the balloon with **15** dots **yellow**. Color the balloon
with **20** dots **blue**. Color the rest **green**.

Cross off as you count.

Lost and Found

Find and count: **1** hula hoop, **2** dominos, **3** toy balls. Then find and circle the **9** objects in this Hidden Pictures puzzle.

wrench

leaf

spoon

crescent moon

envelope

straw

flashlight

slice of pizza

fish

Forest Dance

In the top picture, find and count: **4** mushrooms, **5** insects, **6** musical notes. Then circle all the differences you see between these pictures.

Ms. Number's House

Find and circle: one 1, two 2's, three 3's, four 4's, five 5's, six 6's, seven 7's, eight 8's, and nine 9's.

Hint: All 9's and 6's are right-side up.

Silly Pet Shop

Circle the cat tower with the most cats. Circle the cubby with the most dogs. Circle the fish bowl with the most fish.

What silly things do you see?

Number Carnival

Find and circle the numbers from 1 to 20 in this scene.

15 Minutes a Day

Congratulations!

_____
(your name)

**worked hard
and finished**

**Kindergarten Success
Number
Puzzles**

Answers

Page 3
Zero Groceries

Page 5
Giddy-Up!

Page 6
Two Socks

Page 7
Double Diner

Page 8
Three Paths

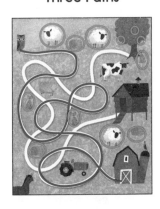

Page 9
Four Sides

Page 10
Five Snacks

Page 11
Six Hats

Page 12
Seven Airplanes

Answers

Page 13
Eight Cats

Page 14
Nine Ants

Page 15
Ten Bikes

Page 16
Fruitful Fives

Page 17
Count Your Chickens

Page 18
Eleven Boats

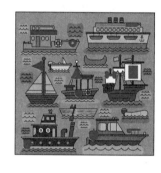

Page 20
Twelve Doughnuts

Page 21
At the Market

Page 22
Thirteen Kids

Page 24
Fifteen Butterflies

46

Answers

Page 25
Super Seal

Page 26
Sixteen Leaves

Page 27
Seventeen Bees

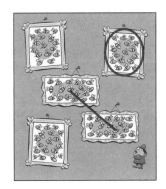

Page 28
Eighteen Hedgehogs

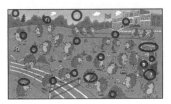

Page 30
Good Morning!

Page 31
Twenty Owls

Page 32
Caterpillar Count

Page 36
What Is It?

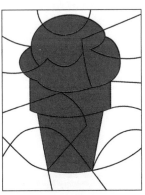

It's an ice-cream cone!

Page 37
Here I Come!

Answers

Page 38
A Bunch of Color

Page 39
Lost and Found

Page 40
Forest Dance

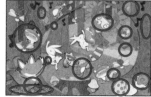

Page 41
Ms. Number's House

Page 42
Silly Pet Shop

Page 43
Number Carnival

Inside Back Cover
Scavenger Hunt